AF483755

VOLUME TWO

EVIL MONKEY MEMES!
VOLUME TWO
BY N BLAKE SEALS
ARTWORK BY BUTCH MAPA & MAURICIO LEONE

EDITED BY VINCENT FERRANTE
DESIGN AND EDITORIAL PRODUCTION BY BLAKE

EVIL MONKEY MEMES! VOLUME TWO PUBLISHED BY MONARCH COMICS.
ISBN 979-8-9894602-2-9
©2023 MONARCH COMICS, LLC./EMM HOLDINGS, INC. ALL RIGHTS RESERVED.
NO PART OF THIS PUBLICATION MAY BE REPRODUCED OR TRANSMITTED IN ANY FORM OR BY
ANY MEANS, EXCEPT SHORT EXCERPTS FOR REVIEW, WITHOUT THE EXPRESS WRITTEN
PERMISSION OF THE AUTHOR OR PUBLISHER.

MONARCHCOMICS.COM

EVIL MONKEY MAN!
IT WAS A SONG. THEN IT WAS A COMIC BOOK. NOW...IT'S A MEME.
ISN'T EVERYTHING?
THE HALLMARK OF TWENTY FIRST CENTURY INSTAGRAM PHILOSOPHY.
THE MEME.

INITIALLY A BY-PRODUCT OF PROMOTING THE COMIC, THESE MEMES,
CREATED FOR FACEBOOK, EVENTUALLY TOOK ON A LIFE OF THEIR OWN.
NOW, WITH HUNDREDS OF THOUSANDS OF LIKES AND SHARES, THEY
DESERVE A BOOK, OR TWO, OF THEIR OWN - EVEN IF IT IS A REALLY LITTLE
BOOK. ONE YOU CAN LEAVE IN THE BATHROOM FOR COMMODIOUS
ENJOYMENT ;)

SO THEN, ONCE AGAIN, IN THE TRADITION OF THE ONE-LINER, THE
IRREVERANT SARCASM OF THE GOTCHA, AND THE ELEVATED ART OF
THE COFFEE TABLE JOKE BOOK...PLEASE ENJOY THIS, THE SECOND
COLLECTION OF *EVIL MONKEY MEMES..!*

ART · MAURICIO LEONE · EMM EPISODE FIVE

THANKS FOR EXPLAINING THE WORD "MANY" TO ME...
...IT MEANS A LOT.

ART · BUTCH MAPA · EMM EPISODE FOUR

DON'T SPELL PART BACKWARD...
...IT'S A TRAP.

ART · BUTCH MAPA · EMM EPISODE FOUR

THERE'S A NEW RESTAURANT CALLED KARMA...
...THERE'S NO MENU. YOU GET WHAT YOU DESERVE.

ART · BUTCH MAPA · EMM EPISODE FOUR

I USED TO THINK I WAS INDECISIVE...
...BUT NOW I'M NOT TOO SURE.

ART · BUTCH MAPA · EMM EPISODE THREE

DID YOU HEAR ABOUT THE GUY WHO GOT HIT IN THE HEAD WITH A CAN OF SODA?
HE DIDN'T GET HURT BECAUSE IT WAS A SOFT DRINK.

ART · BUTCH MAPA · EMM EPISODE THREE

KEEP THE DREAM ALIVE...
...HIT THE SNOOZE BUTTON.

ART · BUTCH MAPA · EMM EPISODE FOUR

I DIDN'T LIKE MY BEARD AT FIRST...
...BUT IT GREW ON ME.

ART · MAURICIO LEONE · EMM EPISODE SIX

HAVE YOU EVER WORRIED...
...THAT YOU'RE JUST SOMEONE ELSE'S IMAGINARY FRIEND?

ART · BUTCH MAPA · EMM EPISODE THREE

WHEN EVERYTHING IS COMING YOUR WAY...
...YOU'RE IN THE WRONG LANE.

ART · MAURICIO LEONE · UNITED FORCES CRASHOVER ISSUE ONE

I WASN'T ORIGINALLY GOING TO GET A BRAIN TRANSPLANT...
...BUT THEN I CHANGED MY MIND.

ART · BUTCH MAPA · EMM EPISODE THREE

I WENT TO BUY CAMOUFLAGE TROUSERS...
...BUT I COULDN'T FIND ANY.

ART · BUTCH MAPA · EMM EPISODE ONE & TWO

I HAVE AN INFERIORITY COMPLEX...
...BUT IT'S NOT A VERY GOOD ONE.

ART · BUTCH MAPA · EMM EPISODE THREE

Remember...
...TODAY IS THE TOMORROW YOU WORRIED ABOUT YESTERDAY.

ART · MAURICIO LEONE · EMM EPISODE SIX

DON'T YOU HATE IT WHEN SOMEONE ANSWERS THEIR OWN QUESTIONS? I DO.
MONARCH COMICS
MONKEY MEME MONDAY

ART · BUTCH MAPA · EMM EPISODE THREE

MY THERAPIST SAYS I HAVE A PREOCCUPATION WITH REVENGE...WE'LL SEE ABOUT THAT.
MONARCH COMICS
MONKEY MEME MONDAY

ART · MAURICIO LEONE · EMM EPISODE SIX

ALWAYS BORROW MONEY FROM A PESSIMIST.
THEY'LL NEVER EXPECT IT BACK.
OPEN
MONARCH COMICS
MONKEY MEME MONDAY

ART · MAURICIO LEONE · EMM EPISODE FIVE

A TERMITE WALKS INTO A BAR AND ASKS,
"IS THE BAR TENDER HERE?"
MONARCH
COMICS
MONKEY MEME MONDAY

ART · MAURICIO LEONE · EMM EPISODE FIVE

MONKEY MEME MONDAY

ART · MAURICIO LEONE · EMM EPISODE FIVE

GIVE A MAN A FISH, YOU FEED HIM FOR A DAY.
TEACH A MAN TO FISH AND YOU SAVED
YOURSELF A FISH, HAVEN'T YOU?
mOnkey meme mondAy
MONARCH
COMICS

ART · MAURICIO LEONE · EMM EPISODE FIVE

I ALWAYS TAKE LIFE WITH A GRAIN OF SALT.
AND A SLICE OF LIME.
AND A SHOT OF TEQUILA.
mOnkey meme MondAy

MONARCH
COMICS

ART · BUTCH MAPA · EMM EPISODE THREE

IT'S HARD TO EXPLAIN PUNS TO KLEPTOMANIACS,
THEY'RE ALWAYS TAKING THINGS LITERALLY.
mOnkey meme
MondAy

MONARCH
COMICS

ART · BUTCH MAPA · EMM EPISODE FOUR

LIGHT TRAVELS FASTER THAN SOUND.
WHICH IS WHY SOME PEOPLE APPEAR BRIGHT,
UNTIL THEY OPEN THEIR MOUTH.
mOnkey meme MondAy

MONARCH
COMICS

ART · BUTCH MAPA · EMM EPISODE THREE

I DON'T HAVE AN ATTITUDE PROBLEM.
YOU HAVE A PERCEPTION PROBLEM.
mOnkey meme MondAy
MONARCH
COMICS

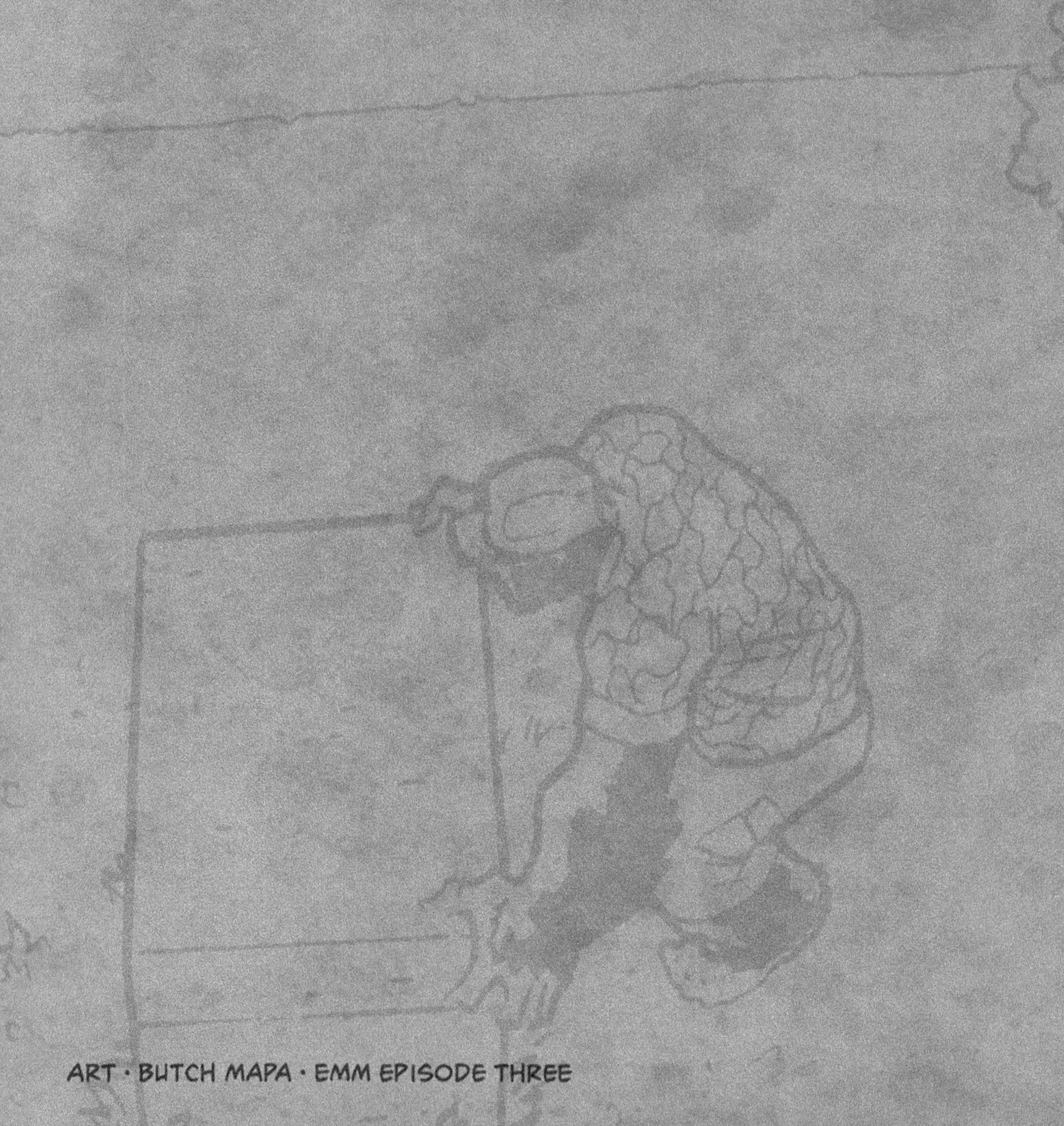

ART · BUTCH MAPA · EMM EPISODE THREE

THERE ARE THREE KINDS OF PEOPLE.

THOSE WHO CAN COUNT
AND THOSE WHO CAN'T.

ART · BUTCH MAPA · EMM EPISODE FOUR

MONARCH
COMICS
mOnkey meme MondAy
I DOUBT, THEREFORE I MIGHT BE.

ART · BUTCH MAPA · EMM EPISODE ONE

LIFE IS LIKE A BIRD.
IT'S PRETTY CUTE UNTIL IT POOPS ON YOUR HEAD.
mOnkey meme
MondAy

MONARCH
COMICS

ART · BUTCH MAPA · EMM EPISODE FOUR

KNOWLEDGE IS KNOWING A TOMATO IS A FRUIT.
eh...
WISDOM IS NOT PUTTING IT IN A FRUIT SALAD.

MONARCH COMICS
monkey meme MondAy

ART · BUTCH MAPA · EMM EPISODE ONE

A COMPUTER ONCE BEAT ME AT CHESS.
BUT IT WAS NO MATCH FOR ME AT KICKBOXING.

MONARCH
COMICS
mOnkey meme mondAy

ART · BUTCH MAPA · EMM EPISODE THREE

WORRYING WORKS!
MORE THAN 90 PERCENT OF THE THINGS
I WORRY ABOUT NEVER HAPPEN.

MONARCH
COMICS
monkey meme
mondAy

ART · MAURICIO LEONE · EMM EPISODE FIVE

MONEY CAN'T BUY YOU HAPPINESS?
WELL, CHECK THIS OUT...
...I BOUGHT MYSELF A HAPPY MEAL.
MONARCH COMICS
mOnkey meme MondAy

ART · BUTCH MAPA · EMM EPISODE FOUR

A POSITIVE ATTITUDE MAY NOT SOLVE
ALL YOUR PROBLEMS...
...BUT IT WILL ANNOY ENOUGH PEOPLE
TO MAKE IT WORTH THE EFFORT.

MONARCH
COMICS
monkey meme
MondAy

EXIT
ART · MAURICIO LEONE · EMM EPISODE FIVE

Alcohol is a perfect solvent.
IT DISSOLVES MARRIAGES, FAMILIES, AND CAREERS.

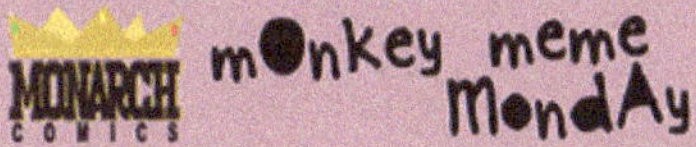
MONARCH COMICS
monkey meme mondAy

ART · MAURICIO LEONE · UNITED FORCES CRASHOVER ISSUE ONE

I GOT A NEW PAIR OF GLOVES TODAY...

...BUT THEY'RE BOTH LEFTS, WHICH, ON THE ONE HAND,
IS GREAT, BUT ON THE OTHER, IT'S JUST NOT RIGHT.

ART · BUTCH MAPA · EMM EPISODE TWO

MONKEY MEME MONDAY

THE BIGGEST PROBLEM WITH STUPID PEOPLE...

...IS THAT THEY'RE NOT DUMB.

ART · MAURICIO LEONE · EMM EPISODE SIX

MONARCH
COMICS
MONKEY MEME MONDAY
If money doesn't grow on trees...
OPEN
...HOW COME BANKS HAVE BRANCHES?

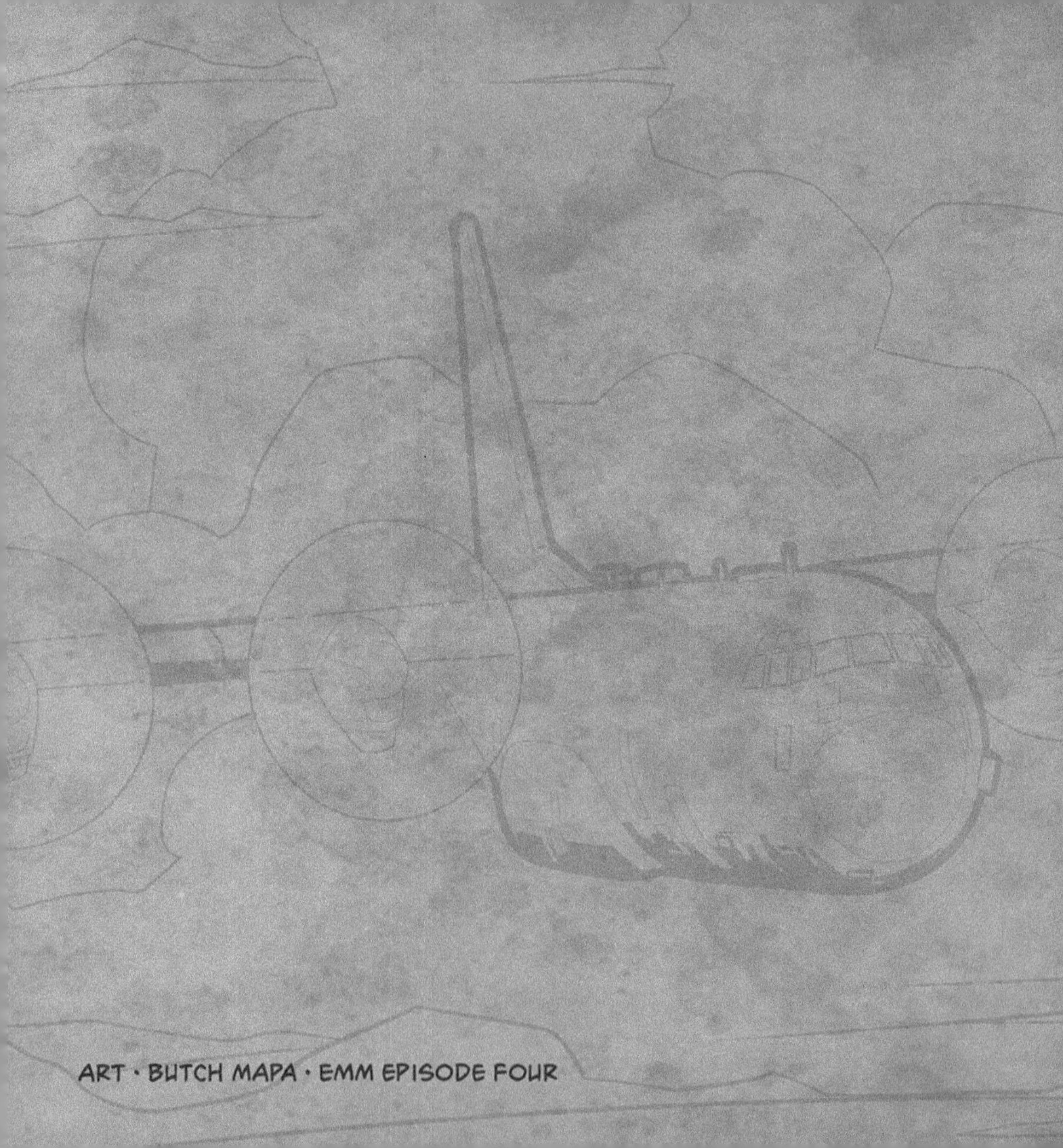

ART · BUTCH MAPA · EMM EPISODE FOUR

MONKEY MEME MONDAY

I bought the world's worst thesaurus...

...NOT ONLY IS IT TERRIBLE, BUT IT'S ALSO TERRIBLE.

ART · BUTCH MAPA · EMM EPISODE TWO

PEOPLE TELL ME I'M CONDESCENDING.

THAT MEANS I TALK DOWN TO PEOPLE.

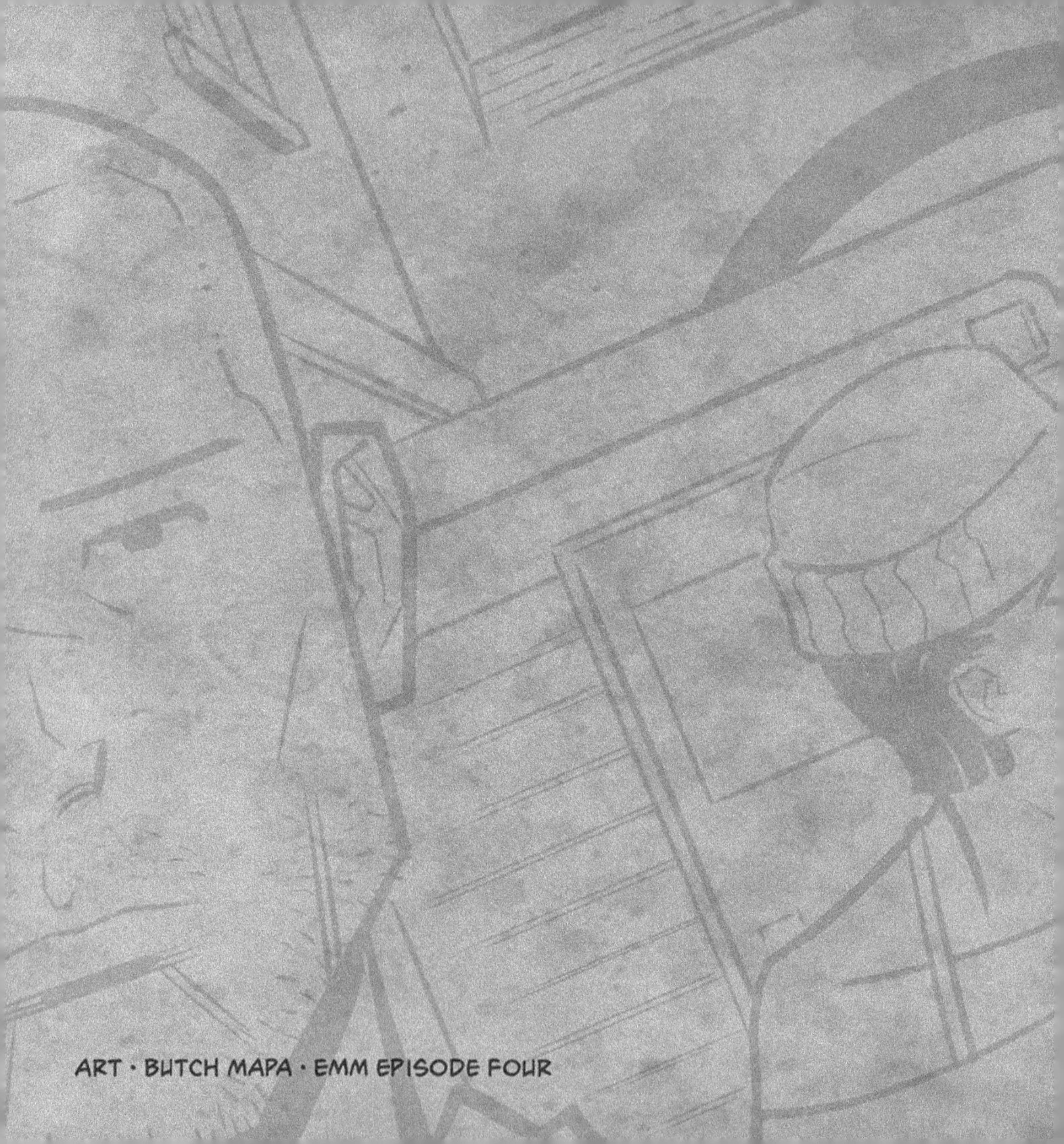

ART · BUTCH MAPA · EMM EPISODE FOUR

MONKEY MEME MONDAY

I HAVE A BUMPER STICKER THAT SAYS
"HONK IF YOU THINK I'M SEXY."

THEN I JUST SIT AT GREEN LIGHTS UNTIL
I FEEL BETTER ABOUT MYSELF.

ART · BUTCH MAPA · EMM EPISODE FOUR

MONARCH COMICS
MONKEY MEME MONDAY
APPARENTLY I SNORE SO LOUDLY THAT IT SCARES
EVERYONE IN THE CAR I'M DRIVING.

ART · BUTCH MAPA · EMM EPISODE FOUR

MONARCH COMICS
I TOLD MY GIRL SHE DREW HER EYEBROWS TOO HIGH.
SHE SEEMED SURPRISED.

ART · BUTCH MAPA · EMM EPISODE THREE

I WANT TO DIE PEACEFULLY IN MY SLEEP
LIKE MY GRANDFATHER.

NOT SCREAMING AND YELLING LIKE
THE PASSENGERS IN HIS CAR.

ART · BUTCH MAPA · EMM EPISODE THREE

MONARCH
COMICS
MONKEY MEME MONDAY
I JUST BURNED 2,000 CALORIES.
THAT'S THE LAST TIME I LEAVE BROWNIES
IN THE OVEN WHILE I NAP.

ART · BUTCH MAPA · EMM EPISODE TWO

MONKEY MEME MONDAY
THE PROBLEM ISN'T THAT OBESITY RUNS IN MY FAMILY...
...THE PROBLEM IS THAT NO ONE RUNS IN MY FAMILY.
MONARCH COMICS

ART · BUTCH MAPA · EMM EPISODE FOUR

YOU DON'T NEED A PARACHUTE
TO GO SKYDIVING...
...YOU NEED A PARACHUTE TO GO
SKYDIVING TWICE.

MONARCH
COMICS

ART · BUTCH MAPA · EMM EPISODE TWO

MONKEY MEME MONDAY
IF YOU SERVE YOUR KIDS FROZEN PIZZA OR CHICKEN NUGGETS...YOU ARE A TERRIBLE PARENT.
I DON'T CARE HOW BUSY YOU ARE, FIND THE TIME TO MICROWAVE THEM.

MONARCH
COMICS

ART · BUTCH MAPA · EMM EPISODE TWO

...WHEN DID COMPUTERS START ASKING HUMANS TO PROVE THAT THEY'RE NOT ROBOTS?!

ART · BUTCH MAPA · EMM EPISODE FOUR

MONKEY MEME MONDAY
I LIKE TO HOLD HANDS AT THE MOVIES...
...WHICH ALWAYS SEEMS TO STARTLE STRANGERS.

ART · BUTCH MAPA · EMM EPISODE THREE

MONKEY MEME MONDAY
MY MATH TEACHER CALLED ME AVERAGE...
...SHE'S SO MEAN!

ART · MAURICIO LEONE · EMM EPISODE SIX

MONKEY MEME MONDAY
THE OTHER DAY I ASKED THE BANKER TO CHECK MY BALANCE...
OPEN
...SO SHE PUSHED ME.

ART · BUTCH MAPA · EMM EPISODE FOUR

MONKEY MEME MONDAY
I CAN'T BELIEVE I GOT FIRED FROM THE CALENDAR FACTORY...
...ALL I DID WAS TAKE A DAY OFF!
2020

FEATURING ARTWORK BY BUTCH MAPA & MAURICIO LEONE
FROM THE SAGA OF EVIL MONKEY MAN! EPISODES 1 - 6
AND UNITED FORCES CRASHOVER ISSUE 1
AVAILABLE AT MONARCHCOMICS.COM

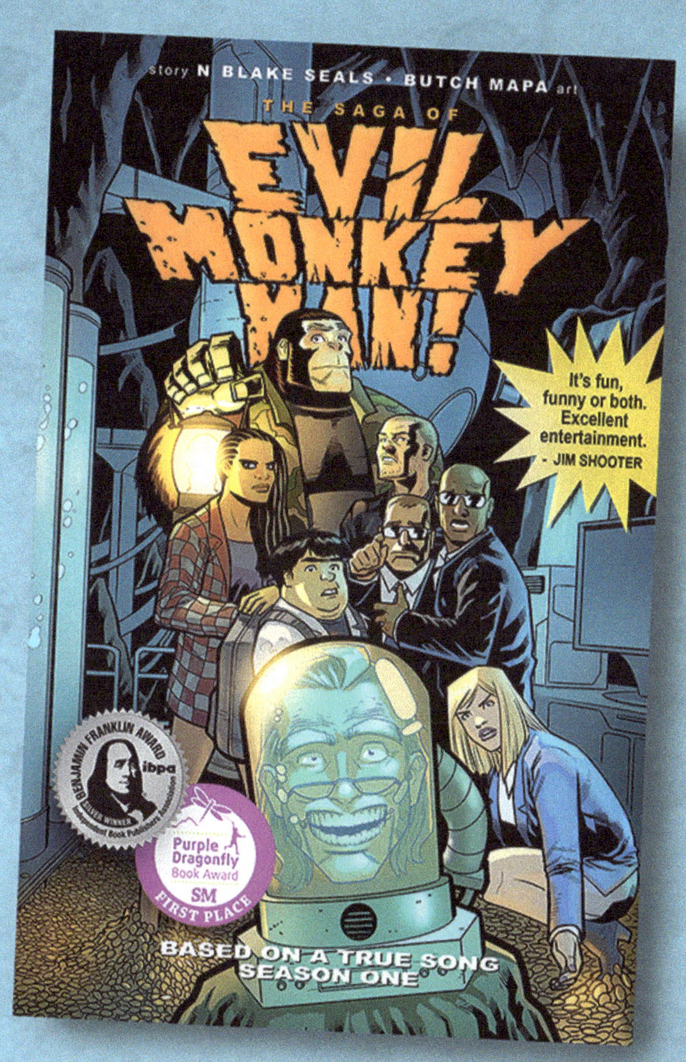

story N BLAKE SEALS • BUTCH MAPA art
THE SAGA OF
EVIL MONKEY MAN!
It's fun, funny or both. Excellent entertainment. - JIM SHOOTER
BENJAMIN FRANKLIN AWARD
ibpa
SILVER WINNER
Purple Dragonfly Book Award
SM
FIRST PLACE
BASED ON A TRUE SONG
SEASON ONE

www.ingramcontent.com/pod-product-compliance
Lightning Source LLC
Chambersburg PA
CBHW042050150726
48005CB00036B/2970